The Chill Panda

Published in 2026 by New Holland Publishers

newhollandpublishers.com

A record of this book is held at the National Library of Australia.

ISBN 9781760798611

Managing Director: Fiona Schultz
General Manager/Publisher: Olga Dementiev
Production Director: Arlene Gippert

Keep up with New Holland Publishers:

NewHollandPublishers
@newhollandpublishers

The Chill

8 LESSONS FOR OVERCOMING

FEAR, STRESS, AND INSECURITY

DURING UNEXPECTED TIMES

Dealing with Change in Work and Life

JOSEPH RODRICK LAW

AUTHOR OF *AUTHENTIC POWER AND GREATNESS*

Foreword

No one more than my friend Joseph Rodrick Law has worked harder at exploring the intersection of modern life and universal teachings on inner peace. This humane and curious man speaks as one who knows in his bones that peace of mind is to be reached exploring ancient wisdom. Yes, there are other books that explore ancient truths in the welter of modernity. But Joseph finds fresh ways to guide us through these paradoxes.

One paragraph lifted from this flow of wisdom makes the point. It might comfort people battered by a shock in their lives, such as bereavement or business setback or family disputes. Says Joseph:

"Sudden change may be a blessing in disguise because it allows us to look at ourselves and our circumstances in entirely new ways. Whenever a sudden change happens to you, be still, and take time to go within. Use such times for deep contemplation, as it may be a golden opportunity to reevaluate your life."

My dear reader, don't dismiss this as fridge magnet wisdom. The simpler the truth, the greater. I am sure there will be people suffering the loss of a partner or child, or a great career upheaval like losing an election or a friendship – or even the advent of war or environmental disaster – who will be induced to think on this. Use such unsettling times for contemplation.

Insists Joseph: maybe you can explore hidden talents and develop them for the long run, become better and stronger – all out of sudden change.

Between his success in business, his fresh thinking on philanthropy, and his appreciation for timeless wisdom of East and West, Joseph makes himself the perfect guide. He reduces these deep explorations to the wholesome simplicity of a story, in which navigating change is the focus – telling us that we can make it even through the darkest, most bewildering times and change our lives for the better.

We can choose action or non-action. And we can choose to walk with harmony, kindness, and integrity.

Take this journey with this wise man.

The Honourable Bob Carr

Former Foreign Minister of Australia
Former Premier of New South Wales

PRAISE FOR JOSEPH RODRICK LAW'S BOOKS

The Chill Panda: Dealing with Change in Work and Life

"Joseph is in search of himself. An earnest and sincere student of spiritual life, he adds value to everyone he comes in contact with. He is wise beyond his age. He has done a marvelous job at taking a complex issue and distilling it down to a simple story, with practical guidance that anyone can follow. It is a must-read for anyone dealing with and managing change."

Ashish Chauhan
CEO of the National Stock Exchange of India
(World's 4th largest stock exchange with a market capitalization of US$5 trillion as at May 2024)

"Joseph is a young man blessed with a deep humanity and sage insights into human nature. His deep understanding of the cultural and philosophical norms of East and West makes him a valuable and enlightened thought leader."

The Honorable Hugo Llorens
Former Ambassador of the United States
to Afghanistan and Honduras

"The Chill Panda has become my spiritual guide in work and life. Reading this book every night gives me so much guidance, awareness and insights, it helps me to go through transformation during this period of difficulty and uncertainty, to rethink, regroup and recreate. I'm amazed by Joseph's wisdom."

Vivienne Tam
International Fashion Designer
Forbes magazine's "25 Top Chinese Americans in Business

"A simple parable revealing a powerful way of transforming stress into a mindful state of calm and presence to make your life more empowered, creative and productive."

Dr John Demartini
International best-selling author of
The Values Factor and author of 40 books

"Everyone deserves a Chill Panda in their life. It's essential for personal growth, work, and overall well-being. Chill Panda has helped me conquer my fears, stay calm in challenging situations, and embrace the present moment.

Chill Panda isn't just a book or a character. It represents a mindset and valuable wisdom. I'm truly grateful for the chance to learn from Chill Panda, which has significantly enhanced my mental preparation for training and competitions."

Grace Mo Sheung Lau
World #1 Karate Kata Champion
Tokyo 2020 Olympic Games Medalist
World Games Champion

"Unveil the secrets to inner calm and resilience with "The Chill Panda" by Joseph Rodrick Law. Explore practical strategies for inding balance, purpose, and mindfulness in the face of life's uncertainties. This book is your guide to embracing change, mastering emotions, and cultivating a sense of peace in every aspect of your life."

Suresh Prabhu
Honorable Former Union Minister of Civil Aviation, Railways, Commerce & Industry, Government of India
Guest Professor of London school of Economics

"The Chill Panda is an exceptional book that I highly recommend to anyone seeking happiness and relief from everyday stress. Joseph delivers profound wisdom in a simple and accessible manner, guiding readers on a journey of self-discovery."

Dr Angélica Anglés
Planetary scientist & Astrobiologist, Analogue Astronaut

"I personally found that this book provides the reader with a simple way of breaking down some of life's more difficult challenges and through your story-telling Joseph, you have found a unique way to guide us as we think through and consider an approach to address our own issues."

Peter Liddell
Partner - Asia Pacific Head of Strategy and Operations
KPMG Australia

"If you are looking for a more powerful and creative life, never miss Joseph's writings!"

Sandy Cher
General Manager of Marie Claire Magazine

"Humans like Joseph are one of a kind. He is a simple (Chill) and a superior (Panda) being at the same time. Being a millennial myself, being at peace with your inner self is crucial for personal development in this ever-changing chaotic world. I firmly believe his work resonates with humans of all ages and is key for spiritual self-growth at any stage of your life. More power to you, my friend, brother, & mentor."

HRH King Chaitanya Raj Singh Bhati of Jaisalmer
(159th lineal descendant of Lord Krishna)

"I have known Joseph for more than a decade. He is an accomplished man, yet humble, and deeply engaged in philanthropy.

It took me many decades to grasp the lessons Joseph conveys in just eight chapters. If only I had access to this wisdom earlier, it would have spared me much trial and error. A timeless guide for anyone seeking wisdom and peace in a busy world."

Babak Moini
Co-founder, Laser Clinics Australia & Skinstitut
(Laser Clinics was sold to global private equity firm KKR for AUD $650 million)

"Joseph has a sincere and passionate desire to help others and to make the world a better place."

Jack Canfield
Co-creator of the Chicken Soup for the Soul® series
#1 New York Times Bestseller
(Author of 500 Million Books Sold Worldwide)

"When I was younger, I remember every teenage fight would either start or end with "chill out!" And as much as it sounds childish, I realize now the importance of relaxing in the midst of anger, frustration, or when faced with changes that are hard to swallow.

There are so many "quotable" items in this book, but instead of telling you what they are here, maybe I'll just let you pick them out yourself after you read it."

Grace Chan
Actress, Television Host, and Miss Hong Kong

"The Chill Panda was a great read that highlighted some very relevant aspects of the nature of everyday life that we all come across in one way or another. It's a story that can be read by all ages and everyone can get something out of it."

Dr John Zakos
Honorary Professor
Faculty of Engineering and IT
University of Technology Sydney

"The precious encounter of Tom and Chill Panda takes me on a journey to discover my inner self. This book nourishes my mind and stimulates my thoughts in the midst of my busy life."

Lambert Chan
Former Chief Executive
Hong Kong Committee for UNICEF

"Joseph is genuine and down to earth. His book is extremely insightful and would help to provide readers to look at life more holistically and put views in perspective."

Lemuel Lee
Managing Director
Head of Wealth Management
BNP Paribas

"To make our world a better place, we need more wisdom, more compassion, more love, more kind people and more good books. That's exactly why we need Joseph and his book."

Louis Cheung
Actor & Singer-Songwriter
Kay Tse
Singer & Actress

"The Chill Panda allows you to easily open the door to wisdom. While we constantly strive to satisfy our desires in life, it is crucial to discover our true wants and achieve inner peace. When faced with adversity, wisdom is the key to overcoming difficult situations."

Dr. Christy Wo
Founder & CEO
Crisathena and IFUBO

"Joseph vividly illustrates profound living wisdoms through The Chill Panda. This book offers a completely new perspective to deal with daily obstacles and stress."

Keith Ng
Executive Director
Morgan Stanley

**This book is dedicated to my family,
whose unconditional love and unwavering
faith in me make everything possible.**

Table of Contents

Embarking On A New Journey

Every year during the winter solstice, children gathered around Tom for a story. Tom had been telling stories to generations of children for years; stories he had heard that piqued his curiosity. Particularly one. This unique story is based on a mythological narrative of the mystical mountain. Therein lies an eternal treasure of wisdom and power, it has been said, that is guarded by a custodian, the wise panda.

One day he finally summoned up his courage to embark on a new adventure to discover the truth about this wise panda, perhaps to gain more tales to tell the children upon his return. Perhaps just to see if this wise panda existed and discover the wisdom and power behind it.

Tom had always enjoyed Eastern cultures and their ancient wisdom that went back thousands of years. As a boy, filled with dreams and aspirations, he took up hiking, but as an active and busy adult with demanding work, family responsibilities, and a busy lifestyle, he often felt tired and overwhelmed. The harsh and practical realities of life often left him disappointed and in despair. Still, telling stories to the children always made him feel more alive.

It had been years since he had taken any time off work for himself. He reasoned that a short time away would do him good, so he decided to escape from the hustle and bustle of city life and find time for a little quietness. He hoped to find the motivation to make some necessary changes to his hectic life and to get away from the disappointments and unexpected changes that were wearing him down.

So on a bright and sunny day, he began his hike up the mountains.

He loved the pandas and had read that there are fewer than 2000 pandas remaining, scattered and vulnerable; an endangered species that lived in bamboo forests high in the mountains of China, and on rare occasions, one might be able to see them.

Over the years, his faith had always propelled him forward with the belief in a better tomorrow. At the same time, he was anxious to transcend mundane living and find a life filled with joy, meaning, and purpose. He felt constrained by his conditions, and unable to escape from the treadmill of everyday living, yet in his heart, he knew somehow things could work out.

For the moment, he wanted to take life easy and ignore his emotions and problems by simply burying them so he wouldn't have to deal with them. He knew it wouldn't make them go away, but at least he would be able to enjoy his time in the great forest searching and hoping to meet the wise panda.

As Tom continued his walk, he felt a sense of inner peace and contentment, feelings that perhaps were long forgotten. At the entrance to the mountain, there stood three panda statues, one with its mouth covered, another with its ears covered, and the last with its eyes covered.

Tom looked at the statues with reverence, understanding that this must be a place sanctified with purity, as indicated by the pandas' unspoken message to speak, hear, and see no evil. He bowed to the pandas and then entered into silent prayer.

As Tom wandered around the forest, enjoying the magnificent scenery of nature, he realized that for a very long time, he had not appreciated such simple pleasures; like melodious birds in trees, or water slithering across rocks at the bottom of a creek. Tom wanted to feel that kind of joy again. He wanted to regain his innocence for the beauty and simple things of life.

Tom started his walk early in the morning. Losing track of time, he gradually ascended his way to the top of the mountain. During the hike, he began to regain some of his much-lost tranquility and peace. His spirit was higher than ever, and he was deeply at peace with himself.

He was not sure how many hours he had hiked when he came across a beautiful river alongside a cave, so he stopped to rest and take a sip of water. As he filled his bottle from the crystal river and looked at his reflection, he realized how peaceful he was.

When he looked across the horizon to another mountain, visible from where he stood, he marveled at the wonder and magnificence of nature.

As Tom reached for his mobile phone so he might capture this most memorable majestic scene, he realized he had lost it somewhere along the path.

Tom found himself lost in the forest and roaming around without direction. His mind became agitated; he had only planned to go for a day hike, but now he was frustrated because he had lost his way. As his mind became more restless, his tranquility now gone, he saw the shadow of a bear and his worry quickly turned into fear.

When he looked closer, he saw that it was a panda. His emotions swung like a pendulum as he went from one extreme to another. He sighed in relief and at the same time experienced great joy, excited to meet with the panda, and fascinated by the bamboo forest. Where had it come from? A moment ago, he was standing by the river's edge, now the forest surrounded him. Little did he realize this unusual encounter would be a springboard for a new phase of his life, one of great self-understanding.

"I thought you were a bear there in the shadows and I was nervous until I saw your black and white fur, so I know you are the wise panda."

The panda rolled on the ground, greatly absorbed in the joy of the moment and playing with the bamboo. The feeling of joy and content overwhelmed him as he rolled back and forth in a playful manner. The panda did not respond.

"Excuse me, may I disturb you?" Tom standing there peered down at the panda.

"Who are you?"

"My name is Tom." Tom bent down to be a little closer to the panda.

"Nice to meet you, Tom. My name is Elvis. Welcome to my home! Don't you worry! We pandas don't roar like other bears. Just relax and enjoy yourself! What brought you here?"

Tom was now excited, having realized his dream of meeting one of the wise pandas. "For many years I have wanted to take this adventure. Partly to renew my strength and spirit through nature, and partly with the hope of meeting you, the wise panda. I was also hoping to return home with some new stories to tell the children about treasures that have been kept secret by custodian, the wise panda."

"So you like to tell stories, hey? Do you like to hear them as well?"

"Yes, indeed, I do like to hear stories."

"Some say I am a custodian of the treasure. I am merely holding the keys to the doorway because the treasure is held in the heart of every person. The treasure you seek is not without, but within."

Tom reflected for a moment before speaking again. "Elvis, by the way, do you know your way around here? I would like to get out of this mountain before it gets dark."

"You know, we pandas are unlike our brothers and sisters in the bear family. We do not hibernate during the winter. Instead, we go down the mountain to find warmer weather. We tend to stay around places where bamboo exists in great supply and abundance." The panda continued to talk as it chewed on another bamboo.

"We have sensitive ears and a good sense of smell, but our eyesight is poor. In fact, our baby cubs are born blind. So what we do and where we go is driven by instinct and intuition.

"You humans have great eyesight and can look afar. I guess if we cooperate, you may be able to find your way out of this mountain. You use your analytical mind, and I'll use my instincts."

"Okay, I will take your lead and we will cooperate together."

"Very well, I will let instinct be my guide. But before we go further, may I offer you a word of caution? Be aware that there are no guarantees along the way, and you may encounter different animal friends."

"Like lions and snakes?"

"Tom, I'm not sure about that. Don't worry, though. We pandas may look lazy, but we're excellent climbers and swimmers. We also have great strength. I can protect you if the need arises."

Tom was concerned because he was not sure how far he had come up the mountain. But in the spirit of cooperation, and with his desire to spend more time getting to know the wise panda, he agreed.

"Elvis, I see that you pandas feed almost exclusively on leaves, stems, and shoots of bamboo."

"We are quite laid back and happy enough to chomp away on bamboo!" the panda responded as he chewed another bamboo shoot. "I don't know what it's like to be human, but I can tell you this. When you are too busy doing, you have no time for being. Being in the moment brings you deep peace and joy."

Elvis paused and looked at Tom to be sure he was absorbing what was being said. "Perhaps you are trying too hard to be accepted instead of looking at and accepting who you are and your gifts. And you surely have gifts, but perhaps you don't recognize them as such. Being fully present allows you to stay calm and relax. You must make peace with yourself and transcend all your negative emotions to a place of acceptance and love. This is what has drawn you to this day, to this adventure. As you continue your journey, you will find your answers."

8 LESSONS
FOR OVERCOMING FEAR, STRESS, AND INSECURITY DURING UNEXPECTED TIMES

LESSON 1

Finding Inner Peace And Happiness

Elvis was a quiet soul. He enjoyed his solitude and his own company and found no enjoyment in chasing after things he didn't need, perhaps except bamboo.

Tom was afraid of being alone. This was the source of all his unhappiness. "Although I am surrounded by people at work, my family, and the children, I often feel so lonely. I lost my mobile phone, and without it, I cannot connect to my family and friends. Why don't you have a problem being alone, all the way up here at the top of a mountain?"

"Pandas greatly enjoy solitude and being alone, but they are never lonely. I enjoy nature, the winds, trees, butterflies, and the fragrant scents of flowers. Actually, we use scent markers to avoid one another!" Elvis laughed. "We prefer solitary living. There is a difference being alone and being lonely. You cannot live alone?" Elvis asked, trying to console Tom.

"I prefer being surrounded by family and friends."

"When you cannot live alone, you cannot make peace with self. When you cannot make peace with yourself, you will end up feeling lonely. All that you experience as happiness will only be fleeting emotions that come and go." The panda's eye twinkled with wisdom.

"Yes, it's very true." Tom took the words of the wise panda deeply to heart and contemplated them. He continued. "Here it's different. I am alone, but I am living in joy and focusing on the moment.

"But I generally have regret about the past and worry about the future. I used to be quite proud of my possessions, which took me a lifetime of hard work to acquire. Here I have no position, money, and even my name is not important, yet I feel a sense of freedom. Back in the modern world, I have so much worry about my health, money, even fear of losing my job. I worry about the opinion of others." Tom paused for a moment, observing the wise panda in all of its strength, simplicity, grace, and wisdom.

Elvis then said, "Learn to be more conscious of your emotions and how they affect your body and mind. Positive feelings and emotions, such as love, caring, kindness, forgiveness, honesty, and gratitude will strengthen your mind. On the other hand, negative emotions such as the feeling of helplessness, denial, anger, resentment, jealousy, greed, and fear will weaken your mind.

"The mind needs to be developed, trained, and disciplined over time. You need to be conscious of your thoughts and emotions. It is only by developing awareness that you will then be able to minimize and eradicate the negativity and transform it with more positive thoughts and emotions."

HAPPINESS

"Occasionally I see a few humans here and there. You all seem to be so busy running around all the time," said the wise panda as he and Tom sat in a clearing in the bamboo trees, enjoying the sun. "How do you humans live? What makes you happy?"

"We become happy when our relationships are good and nurturing," said Tom, who was enjoying listening to the stream gurgle alongside the meadow where they sat.

"What else?"

"When we have a nice home and a career. Those are some of the things that can make us happy."

"Then what else?"

"When we make good money, when we are in good health... "

"Wait," Elvis interrupted. "What happens when you don't have these things?"

"Um... I guess we will not be happy or as happy as we would like to be."

"There seem to be many conditions before you experience happiness. Humans could be a vexation at times. They were supreme creatures, but so unsure of themselves and their abilities, and they always seemed to be searching for happiness."

"Yes, I guess." Tom was fond of the panda and respected his judgment.

"Do all of you humans have these conditions?"

"Everyone has their own set of conditions."

"So you will only be happy if and when certain criteria are met?"

"Hmmm. I guess so. I never really thought about it," replied Tom.

"Your happiness is based upon fulfilling expectations set up by your mind, something that will take place in the future. My happiness, however, comes from focusing on the present. Humans and pandas are so different. We are simpler, we can be happy for no reason simply because we want to be happy, while your happiness is based upon fulfilling a set of conditions and expectations. Just learn to be happy, without conditions or reasons.

"Just as we pandas are generally joyful, you humans are accustomed to being in doubt and worry. You may think it's a norm until you break the pattern and develop a new habit, behavior, or way of life. And until you do that, you remain stuck in a maze, continually looking for a way out of your situation, looking externally for some happiness."

“I really appreciate your generous and insightful guidance.” Tom smiled as he continued to be amazed by the panda’s endless wisdom.

"The secret to happiness is giving with a pure heart, without expecting anything in return. When you have love, kindness, and compassion in your heart, it radiates out to all those you meet. Remember this: as you share happiness, you multiply happiness."

PEACE OF MIND

As Tom followed the panda, he tried to catch his breath as they continued to find their way out, though he tried to maintain his composure.

Tom was the first to speak. "My life seems so endlessly busy. Is it possible for me to experience peace of mind?"

Elvis chewed on another bamboo before replying. "Yes of course. First of all, you need to understand what peace of mind is. Peace of mind is not a passive, idle mind but rather a calm, creative, and resourceful mind that is free from worry, fear, and anxiety. With peace of mind, you will be in a better frame of mind to solve your problems, whatever it may be."

"Now your mind is restless and turbulent. Like the waves of an ocean that comes and goes. Your mind is jumping from thought to thought, with little attention span. When your mind is restless, your heart will not have time for peace. You have to learn to the art of attaining peace of mind.

"Instead, who you are is not the waves, which are ever-changing, but the depth and vastness of the ocean, which is forever deep and eternal.

"The key to peace of mind is acceptance and contentment. Be grateful for what you have. Also, sometimes, when you accept you will never have peace of mind. Peace of mind emerges by your mere fact of accepting it.

"Another key to developing mental and emotional equilibrium in life is to adopt an attitude of expecting the unexpected. If you expect things to go smoothly all the time, you will inevitably meet with stress and anxiety."

"In my world," said the panda between mouthfuls of bamboo, "my most prized possession is my bamboo. What's your most prized possession?"

Tom thought about it for a moment. "I guess in our world, apart from our loved ones, it's money, gold, and gemstones."

"Great," said the panda. "If that's your most important possession, how do you safeguard it, like how we safeguard our bamboo?"

"We keep it in banks and safes to protect it from thieves."

Elvis nodded and chewed and nodded and chewed some more. "Those are your tangible assets. Meanwhile, your mind is your most important intangible asset, because your state of mind determines how you feel in any given moment. It determines your happiness and peace of mind.

"To develop self-mastery and take your life back in control, firstly, you need to be more aware and vigilant of what comes to mind, like having a guard that protects your treasures. Don't let other people or external circumstances easily affect you. Maintain an inner equilibrium so that fear and panic don't harm you.

"Guard your mind against external pressures by filtering out the world's negativities. Maintain balance and harmony by not reacting excessively to external circumstances.

"To change how you think and feel, you can redirect the focus of your mind by asking more empowering questions. At times, and even in great emotional turmoil, ask yourself what you can learn from this experience and how you can become a better person because of it. This will induce a stronger and more positive state of mind. Soon you will realize it may be a blessing in disguise."

"Oh, I never thought about it this way before!" Tom said. "Generally in life, we follow routines and do what we are told, and we generally don't deviate from it. We follow it mechanically, but we never question it. Just like how we live our normal lives."

Elvis then said, “What is normal may not be natural. What is natural may not be normal.

Tom contemplated these words for a moment.

“I am very happy because there are plenty of things here to keep me occupied and entertained!” The panda laughed and laughed at his observation. Even Tom found it somewhat comical.

“Like what?” asked Tom, for all he could see was the stream, the bamboo, and the meadow. There were no people, no activity, no phones, buildings, or stores.

“Nature, sun, moon, and anything from a bee to a lion!”

“Oh, my! Is there a lion in this forest?” Tom was starting to become nervous.

“You will be fine; let’s continue our journey.” With compassionate eyes of understanding, Elvis tried to console Tom and make him feel relaxed.

“Sometimes you feel happy, sometimes sad, but the most important thing is balance and to experience peace of mind. By cultivating even-mindedness, happiness and sorrow, profit and loss, triumph and failure do not disturb your peace of mind.”

LESSON 2

How To Find Your Purpose In Life

"There are certain joys I derive from life," Tom continued, "yet, in general, my life looks quite mechanical and I feel stuck. I have never conveyed this to anyone, not even the people closest to me. Deep down, I aspire for higher living, the pursuit of my dreams, meaning, and a higher purpose.

"I have spent most of my life caring for others, working hard, paying my bills, raising a family, and being on time with my mortgage payments, yet I pay little attention to my own needs and wants; my personal desires and dreams. I buried my dream and heart's desire so I could get on with a so-called normal life, keeping up with society's expectation of what is expected of me."

The panda listened attentively, and Tom was relieved to find a wise and caring friend in Elvis.

"You should do something because you want to do it, not because it's expected by society. When you choose do something, you enjoy it. When you feel obligated to do it, you have stress. Although there are always times when we need to do things to survive. For me, I need to find the bamboo, but I don't stress about finding it.

"When you are living your life mechanically, performing your daily routines without purpose, a part of you dies. Infuse what you do with a sense of meaning and a greater purpose." The panda continued his discourse as his eyes twinkled with deep knowledge.

"Do something that gives you joy. Therein lies the key to living your life's purpose. Finding out 'why' you do something is more important than the 'how'. The 'why' links to your purpose, and it will fuel and motivate you to do great things."

Tom smiled, amazed at the panda's insight. He paused for a short time before gathering his thoughts and then asked for further clarity. “How do we find our purpose?”

The panda nodded, slowly and thoughtfully, before responding. “Your purpose comes from your passion. You find purpose in your life and your work by identifying what ignites your passion. Your purpose in life comes from what drives you from within, what you are enthusiastic about doing. It dwells within the depths of your heart and soul.

"What do you do well? What makes you happy? What are you passionate about? From that stems your purpose. Your unique voice in the world. From your purpose, your destiny unfolds. From that, comes success, as well as your best work."

"When you perform the greatest work, when it is done out of passion and purpose, you will be blessed with energy and excitement for great undertakings and accomplishments. Always remember that extraordinary achievement comes from extraordinary psychology. It is worthwhile to take time to go within and ask yourself 'why' – why are you doing what you are doing? You will be renewed and invigorated with new hope, enthusiasm, and energy.

"The unfoldment of your life's purpose expresses itself inside-out, based on your passion – whatever motivates you, inspires you, and brings you joy when you are immersed in it."

The panda continued, "You do not choose your passions – your passions choose you. Each of us is unique. What is natural for one person may not be so for another. Take time to discover and develop your own gift so that you can share it with others in a meaningful way." And with that, the panda closed his eyes and entered into his realm of peace and tranquility.

Tom remembered once again his childhood dreams and aspirations, long forgotten but still buried in the deep chambers of his heart. He had been ignoring many of his feelings over the years, afraid of communicating with others because he felt the need to get on with life.

"I think I understand," said Tom. "Hmmm. I'd never thought about it that way, and you may be right about that. But I am worried what others will think of me."

"Don't be distressed about what others think about you. What others think about you is their opinion, which you have no control over. Focus on what you can control instead, that is, your character. Who you are is defined by your qualities and character, and how you live your life. The more you conquer negative qualities within you while cultivating good qualities, the more your character develops and strengthens.

"Also, there is no need to compare yourself to another person. You are all unique in your individual ways. Think about how you can share your unique talent and gift with the world. Finding your unique voice in this world may take time, as well as developing it to maturity. Just like everything in nature, it takes time. A tree takes years to grow from a tiny sprout to a big tree."

Tom closed his eyes as well, eager to find his purpose through peaceful contemplation.

LESSON 3

Attaining Balance And Equilibrium

"I have another question, but I'm concerned I might be asking too many questions."

"You can never ask too many questions," Elvis said.

"Actually, I admire and love the color of your fur. I have always loved pandas since I was a small child. Why the color of your fur is so uniquely black and white?"

"Because I spend half of my time sleeping, and the other half eating!" The panda giggled uncontrollably, rolling around on the ground.

“Honestly, my fur is a symbolic representation of the world we live in. It’s about the dualistic nature we see in this world. For example, hot and cold, high or low, good or bad, day and night. Balance is what is needed in the world, and equilibrium in all things.

“I see that with your modern developments, you have begun to neglect the beautiful, magnificent, and healing powers of nature. There must be balance in all things; just as day must follow night, night must follow day.”

“Oh I see,” said Tom. “I learned that in the ancient eastern traditions, they call this the yin and yang, represented by the black and white color.”

“Yes, you can call it that. The balance of yin and yang is embedded in all things we see in this world. And to me, what’s most lovely about it is that it represents the color of my fur!

“My fur represents the magic and embodies the grandiosity of this magnificent world in polarity! Life can be good or bad, and it’s all but an integral part of existence as we know it! You may not be happy to be trapped here, but on the other hand, you are enjoying yourself as well through learning about nature. Balancing yin and yang also means attaining equilibrium in the spiritual and material aspects of life.”

The two sat quietly for a brief moment.

"What do you mean by spiritual and material aspects?" asked Tom.

"Spiritual represents your heart, and material represents the mind. Your heart is your conscience, and your mind is your intellect. Don't live a one-sided life while neglecting the other when you focus solely on the material while forgetting the spiritual, and vice versa. To make peace, your philosophy of life needs to be all-encompassing and strike a balance between the spiritual and material aspects of life.

"So do not repel one over the other, for opposing forces are a natural phenomenon in this world, like the balancing of yin and yang. You cannot live a positive life by neglecting the negativities in life, for they are two sides of the same coin. Without villains in the world, there could be no heroes, and vice versa.

"Life itself is the greatest teacher, and nature is your best friend. You have to learn to make peace with yourself. So you live in the world but are detached at the same time."

Tom thought for a moment, not sure he was correctly grasping what Elvis had just said. "So does it mean we detached from the world altogether??"

"No, that's not the point. Remember my fur, black and white? There is an intricate balance in all things, and both are equally important. Balance is the key. When we look at the bird, it is flying in the sky, like the dreams we aspire to reach. When we look at the tree, it remains firmly grounded. Much like our dreams, which, although aspirational, must be practical and grounded with reason at the same time.

"So to be successful, you need to incorporate both the spiritual aspect and material aspect of your life. My body and black and white fur are nothing but a miniature version of the universe. I see the world by observing the rhythms of my own body, for we are a part of nature. You are as well.

"In fact, to live well, you have to balance different areas of yourself, from physical, mental, emotional to spiritual, as well as your life. And life itself has seasons and rhythms which we must also observe. In the forest, we live harmoniously with each other, and nature has its unique way of regenerating itself through the cycles and rhythms of life."

Tom was pleased with his answers. The panda squealed and clapped his paws with delight.

LESSON 4

Mastering Emotions And Overcoming Fear

"Before we head further, let me warn you: this is the most notorious section of the forest," says the panda giggling.

"Wow, there is a snake!" cried Tom. He began to tremble with intense fear. "Will it bite?"

"Calm down, Tom," said Elvis. "You should be flexible like the grass when instead you are now rigid like the tree! As cuddly as we may look, we are strong and can protect ourselves. We are gentle yet strong."

The snake crawled by and made its way back to the rock.

“Our snake friend teaches us a lot as well,” said Elvis. “You can observe its rhythm. The snake moves in grace, flexible while being alert, deeply focused on the moment.

ERADICATING FEAR

“I feel a bit hungry,” Tom said to Elvis.

The panda picked some wild berries and passed them to Tom. “Enjoy these.”

“Thanks, but are they safe to eat? I’m not sure if they contain any bacteria or viruses.”

“Viruses of the body can be cured. Viruses of the mind, particularly in the form of fear, must also be cured. Just as your body may vomit or produce diarrhea to cleanse and heal, your mind also requires cleansing and healing.

“When you’re afraid, you can’t think logically, and you don’t necessarily act your best. You won’t make the right decision when you panic and become reactive to circumstances. Instead, learn how to calm your mind, stay centered, and chill out at times. Be a master of your mind and emotions. Don’t act or say things out of impulse, especially those you will regret later. Relax, take a breath, close your eyes, take it easy, loosen up, let go, calm down."

The panda continues to explain.

"What's important isn't living in a complete absence of fear but rather triumphing over it. What's the antidote for fear, panic, and insecurity? The first step in overcoming fear is becoming aware of it. A cave that has been dark for hundreds of years can be brightened instantaneously by the presence of sunlight. Awareness can be likened to light, whereas unawareness can be likened to darkness. If you are unconscious or try to bury the emotion, it will continue to weaken and control you.

"To overcome your fear, you need to face what you fear. Mentally, think about the worst case scenario. Imagine it fully and completely, then accept the outcome, whatever it may be. When you make a conscious effort to do this, you realize the situation is not life or death after all. Full unconditional acceptance will bring you peace and harmony.

"On the other hand, your inner resistance will create tension in your body and mind. Face and address your fear with the power of your awareness and conscious presence. Be present. Learn to break unconscious thought patterns and emotions."

Tom contemplated his words for a moment before speaking. "But sometimes we have situations we feel we have no control over. What can we do?"

"If you cannot change a situation, just change your attitude towards it. For our feeling is governed by our belief towards reality. It is a subjective experience.

"Luckily, your thoughts and emotions can be changed by consciously deciding to change them. What you feel about something, whether positive or negative, will always depend on your attitude, your perception, and your willingness to see things through a different lens. Learn to change your thoughts by questioning your belief, so that you can change your reality and what you experience."

"Your perception affects how you see the world," said Elvis. But perception is not fixed. Your perception is a subjective experience based upon your belief. If you always see the world through the lens of judgment, there will always be conflict. If you see the world with eyes of unity, you experience harmony and create unseen opportunities.

The wise panda continued in his philosophy on overcoming fear.

"Faith is the cessation of fear. You need to learn to overcome your fears. You have to have faith in yourself and have the ability to live in the present. Hope and faith sustain us and propel us forward. Have faith in the power of the unseen and what is yet to come. Never lose hope in a brighter tomorrow."

Having just recovered from the initial shock of the snake while continuing to be immersed in their conversation, they saw a shadow.

"There is a lion there hiding among those trees!" cried Tom. "We may become his lunch! What should we do?" He frantically looked from side to side for some sort of shelter where the lion could not reach them.

"When you see a snake or a lion, it triggers deep fear within you, Tom. But I am not too worried by a lion, because we pandas are excellent tree climbers and the lion is not!" chuckled the panda.

"But I am not a good tree climber, either!" cried Tom.

The wise panda remained calm, while Tom trembled. "What will seeing a lion teach us?"

"It will teach us to run for our life!!" laughed the panda.

When Tom looked closer, he realized it was not the shadow of a lion at all, but the shadow of a cat reflected by the sun's light.

"Sometimes, your fears are born out of your imagination. You overcome your fears by facing them and seeing them for what they really are. Dispel your fears, your illusions, once and for all, and take a leap of faith towards the unknown. Achieve your dream by actualizing your true potential."

LESSON 5

Making Peace With Stress And Change

As they continued traveling, Tom began to feel deflated. "How can I get out of this?" Tom panted as they hiked up the alleyway between trees, wandering around in the forest. "I am frustrated because I see myself as an intelligent man and am proud of my abilities, yet I am plagued by fear, worry, and anxiety. Right now, I find myself lost, as I am accustomed to having things around me that I depend on. I find myself becoming agitated by little things, like not having enough food and fatigue."

"Take it easy, Tom, and don't take yourself too seriously. Learn to laugh at your mistakes and your circumstances, for awareness is the first step to the path of change and transformation. You see, every situation is a mirror that will bring out different parts of your inner truth; an unconscious or an unaddressed part of you that may need looking at so you can grow. External events, people, or circumstances stimulate different emotions – the fear, happiness, comfort, or unease within you." The wise panda paused for a moment, looking at Tom to make sure he had his attention.

"We pandas tend to be more chill than you humans, as we only focus on the moment," chuckled the panda. "Sometimes, laziness is the best antidote to what you call stress!"

The panda seemed to doze off before burping softly and rubbing its tummy. After a few minutes the panda said, "I realize you humans constantly think and talk about the past and future. Our concept of time is quite different. To us, time doesn't exist. The past and future don't matter. We focus on the present, eating bamboo, sleeping, and chilling out.

"Sometimes you need to think about the past and future for practical purposes, but too much dwelling on the past and future will create mental tension in your life. Don't dwell in the past. Once you have performed your work, be detached and forgetful. Don't think about the future excessively as well, as this will create unnecessary worry and stress. When you're stressed, it affects not only your mind but your body, and your health deteriorates.

"In fact, your world has become too materialistic. You're constantly in the middle of going somewhere, doing something, or planning for your future."

"Yes, you are right, we humans make time to plan for just about everything, from what time we get up, to what time we eat, work and rest. We rely heavily on clock time."

"We rely solely on biological time," said Elvis. The needs of the body at any given moment are always guided by higher wisdom. When you rely on your so-called clock time, while ignoring your biological time, you feel stressed because you're going against nature. When you respond solely to outer demands, you ignore the wisdom of the body and its rhythm, leading to anxiety and stress.

"The scarcity mindset creates stress and tension in your body and mind. When you feel that you are lacking in something, whether time or money, you create stress and anxiety. On the other hand, when you live with an abundant mindset, feeling you have enough time and enough money, you feel relaxed and calm.

"Learn to enjoy the journey, not just the destination. There's a time for working, just as there are times for relaxing, playing, or simply being without doing anything. Learn to chill. Better yet, just chill!"

DEALING WITH CHANGE

Tom has been particularly anxious and restless as of late due to his work and the fluctuations in the economy, where businesses are collapsing; thus, the security of his job and future looks less certain.

Tom frowned and stared at his shoes. "I feel so insecure. I'm not sure what will happen to me if my job and financial circumstances change because of problems in the economy. With all that afflicts us in the rapidly changing world—the economy, disease, war and natural disasters, I want to be comfortable and not have to put up with changes."

The panda replied, "Do not look for perfection in an imperfect world. Some things will happen all of a sudden, no matter how well you plan. Stay calm and centered at times like this, and don't lose hope. It may be an opportunity for a change and something new in your life."

After that, Elvis appeared to be sleeping. Tom waited a few minutes, glancing from his shoes to its round face. Finally, after a few minutes the panda yawned and said, "First, you need to understand that the world is in a state of constant change. In fact, the only thing that remains unchanged is change. If you develop inner resistance to the inevitability of change, you'll create unnecessary stress and anxiety."

To do this, Elvis recommended looking at life in a new way. "Change is to be embraced and celebrated, not feared. For without ending, there is no new beginning. That's the rhythm of life. Creation, and sustenance, and endings only begin new cycles in life's rhythms."

"Sudden change may be a blessing in disguise because it allows us to look at ourselves and our circumstances in entirely new ways. Whenever a sudden change happens to you, be still, and take time to go within. Use such times for deep contemplation as it may be a golden opportunity to reevaluate your life. Maybe you can explore hidden talents and develop them for the long term. Maybe, you'll come up with your next big dream."

"Old patterns, habits, and routines make life feel dull, mechanical, and bereft of purpose or direction. Create something new. Envision a new you. If you set out on a new adventure, you might see the circumstances of your life in terms of not just what is, but what can be.

"When something new presents itself, no matter how it seems to you at the outset, keep an open mind and see what unfolds. Don't hold rigid views or expectations. That's right. Don't be rigid like the tree; rather, be flexible like the grass. Trees break in strong winds, whereas grass only bends by remaining flexible.

"To make changes, take baby steps, and build momentum over time. Initially, everything will seem difficult as it is an uphill battle, just as it is when we walk towards the top of a mountain. However, it becomes easier when we walk down again, once we've reached the top.

"Finally, remember, you will always play a role in everything that happens in your life. When something doesn't go your way or you don't get what you want, accept that you had some part in the way things turned out. Do not blame others or act like a victim.

"If you feel that you are a victim of a situation and start blaming, this does not serve you; in fact, this weakens you as you are acknowledging that an external force is in control, rather than taking mastery over your own mind and its emotions. This is one of the key lessons in self-understanding and self-mastery. Instead, learn to transcend and transform negative emotion to a place of love, harmony and compassion.

"Perhaps you can begin to think about what you are grateful for in your life. Being grateful for all the things that come your way, even lessons you thought were negative at the time they occurred, opens another door of opportunity. Soon you will realize all your obstacles are nothing but blessings in disguise."

Tom was amazed by the panda's wisdom and realized that even out of suffering, tragedy, and destruction, something of beauty can emerge.

CHANGING YOUR LIFE

With his newfound enthusiasm and courage, Tom asked, "Then how can we change our life for the better in the midst of change?"

"That's a good question, Tom. All people, events, and circumstances are nothing but a mirror that reflects your inner beliefs and temporary state of mind. When you begin to change your thoughts, the circumstances of your life will begin to change.

"Envision a new life, and dare to dream. Your previous thinking has led you to the life you are living now. Don't try to live a new life with old habits and old ways of thinking. Change your old ways of thinking, habits, and routine. To begin a new life, think anew, with a different paradigm and higher level of consciousness. Seek the company of the wise, intelligent, and successful.

"Change is a wake-up call to a new paradigm of life. The old must be replaced to usher in the new. As the world changes, we usher in a new era of fresh hope and advancement."

LESSON 6

The Dichotomy Of Action vs. Nonaction

After Elvis and Tom had their drink from the stream, they continued to wander through the bamboo forest and found themselves in a pine woods. They chatted amiably and continued to contemplate the meaning of life while the wise panda imbued his wisdom to Tom. Soon the two lost track of time.

Finally, as the sun began to set, Tom realized it was time for him to go home. "I want to know how we can get out of these woods," said Tom. "Do we have a plan?"

“I do not have a plan,” replied Elvis. ”Let us enjoy the forest along the way and we will see what unfolds. We don’t plan as you humans do. Rather than thinking with our minds, we tend to go with our instincts. I live one moment at a time and see what unfolds.”

“Are all animals like that?” asked Tom.

“Yes, but some animals do plan. You see our squirrel friends there? They have their nuts stored for winter! Because they eat nuts that are not available to them during the winter, they must prepare so they have enough food to get them through the bare season. We pandas, however, are a different species and we eat what comes along, mainly bamboo!”

“Why do you seem to look more relaxed than I?”

“Your mind is restless because you are too busy doing, seeking, thinking, fearing what the future will hold. Whereas I am just being. I do not anticipate danger. There may be some, but I deal with it when it comes to me, when I sense it, not before. You are guided by your mind, whereas I am guided by my instinct and intuition.”

“I’m not sure I understand the difference,” said Tom. “You deal with danger as it arises, but I have a plan to deal with it when it comes. Isn't that better because I'm always prepared?"

"Being prepared is a good thing. It's based on knowledge. If you know a storm is coming, you should get yourself prepared by finding shelter. But if you constantly try to prepare for any and every event that might take place, but have no basis in fact, you will spend your life preparing for things that will likely never happen.

"In your instance, you live in a different world that requires both planning and spontaneous action arising from the needs at a particular time. This goes back to the black and white color of my fur, the balance in all things. So I guess both are important for you, focusing on your instinct and maintaining adequate planning for your needs. You are a very complex species among animals.

"See our monkey friends there on the top of the tree? The hunters entice the monkeys with a nut in their traps. The monkey smells the nut, comes down from the top of the tree and squeezes his tiny hand through a narrow opening in order to get the nut. Once he grabs the nut, then his fist holding the nut is too big to pass through again. If he dropped the nut, he would be able to remove his hand, but he will not drop the nut, so our monkey friend then loses his freedom for only a small nut!"

Elvis was indeed wise, thought Tom. "I see your point; sometimes we just have to learn to let go of things, which can be seen as larger in value at the time, but which may come with consequences that are more harmful than good."

"I see you've grasped this concept well, Tom." Elvis smiled and nodded.

"In my own life, I often regret the past and have much concern for the future. Sometimes I have anxiety about not having something, and by the time I have it, I fear that it will be taken away from me. So does it mean we should give up striving?" asked Tom.

"No, not at all. It is often the attachment to things or an outcome that creates the anxiety. You can still enjoy the process, but do not be rigidly attached to the outcome. In everything you do, simply perform your best action, but remain detached from the fruit of your labor.

"Having this mindset doesn't mean that you do not care about the outcome, or that you have no goals or expectations. Rather, it means that while you actively work toward a favorable outcome, you remain detached from the factors that you have no control over anyway, once you have done your part. We have to know what we can and can't control, with the wisdom to know the difference. Sometimes we have to plan, and sometimes we need to let go!" Elvis replied.

"Be strong but not rigid.
Be quick but not in a hurry.
Work hard, but do not forget
how to enjoy life.
Take action, but do not be
attached to the outcome."

LESSON 7
Leadership Lessons From Nature

Next to Tom and Elvis, there were a few bees collecting honey from the flowers.

"You see our bee friends there? They collect nectars from different flowers and turn it into honey. Nature is your teacher. So you learn from its wisdom. Like the bees, you take out the nectar of these lessons and embody it into your life.

"They are hardworking; any bee may visit thousands of flowers on any given day, to take nectar and pollen to the hive. The bee works unceasingly for the benefit of all. They are not competitive in this but maintain a spirit of cooperation."

Tom was pleased by the observation of Elvis. "I agree. Their community is both incredibly efficient and harmonious in a way rarely seen in human society. The bee teaches us working unity for the greater good of all. What great lessons for working cooperatively and leadership!"

"Yes! There is also the queen bee. She isn't a tyrannical leader. She is, rather, a servant to her hive; she performs her role in producing more bees so that the hive continues. She is a servant leader. Have you heard the saying you are what you eat!?"

"Yes," replied Tom. "It means eating good food to remain healthy and fit."

"Nowhere is that truer than when it comes to honey bees. Bees that are fed bee bread and honey become female workers, and larvae that become queens are fed only royal jelly. Likewise, when you eat solely on bamboos, you become a panda!"

Tom laughed in agreement and said, "By the way, the honey must be quite tasty!"

"Finally, there is one more thing to note. Don't play with the beehive. We stay away from that!" chuckled Elvis.

After a brief moment, they discovered a nearby stream.

"I am thirsty," noted Tom. Can we drink this water in the stream?"

"Yes! This water is beautiful and clean!

"Water is magnificent because it offers service to all without asking for anything in return. It nurtures and nourishes life. Water is a great example of the balance of yin and yang because it's shapeless, yet it can be turned into many forms."

Tom collected water with his hands as it flowed downstream. "Where does this water go?" he asked.

"The water from this stream flows downs to the sea. Do you know why all streams flow to the sea?"

"Because the sea is situated lower than the stream?"

"Yes, that's the point. The sea lies below them, so it becomes the king of all streams. Like the queen bee example, it is a lesson in leadership."

"Oh I see," said Tom. "What you are trying to tell me is that it is symbolic because as you lead people, you are in another way serving them. A great leader serves others through humility."

Elvis then said. "Yes, we have much to learn from nature. Life is a process of becoming. Think of who you want to become and the qualities you would like to express in this world through learning from nature. Emulate the greatness of nature, such as courage, wisdom, harmony, kindness, gratitude, intelligence, generosity, humility, integrity, and strength, and incorporate these ten qualities into your life. These are qualities that are not only essential for success in leadership but also for success in all of life's endeavors as a human being."

10 Qualities Of The Wise Panda

Courage
Take action toward worthy goals in spite of fear.

Wisdom
Be guided by your heart, conscience, and inner compass.

Harmony
Live at peace with yourself and the world.

Kindness
Be kind to everyone and all living beings.

Gratitude
Be thankful and appreciative for everything in your life.

Intelligence
Develop and harness the mind's potential.

Generosity
Contribute to others without expecting anything in return.

Strength
Exercise your willpower in overcoming difficulties.

Humility
Know that you are no greater than those whom you serve.

Integrity
Be true to and stay congruent with your thoughts, words, and actions.

Tom and Elvis followed the stream as it made its way down the mountain.

"Observe the stream. It does not toil, but finds its way easily by following its natural course."

"But I am not a stream," said Tom.

"You are a human, the greatest of all the animals in many ways. Surely you are able to find your way."

"And look at the beautiful sun!" Elvis went on. "The sun gives and all life on the planet is dependent on it. Like the water, it offers to all but does not expect anything in return. It embodies completely the spirit of selflessness. Like a mother who loves her child unconditionally, it radiates love and warmth to all living beings on Earth.

"The sun, wind, and rain do not discriminate, but equally meet with those they encounter. See the equality and beauty of all, for we are but one big family living in this place called Earth. Learn to live in harmony with each other based upon mutual respect, love, and understanding. In your world, treat others the way you want to be treated. Always exercise kindness, love, and compassion. We should always be growing and contributing to the greater good."

"Look at the vastness of the sky and the clouds. You are the sky, which is clear and infinite in nature. Yet you are constrained by your thoughts and emotions, which are likened to the cloud in the sky. The clouds come and go, and so do your emotions, but forever will you remain like the sky, which is pure, vast, and limitless."

“The moon gradually waxes day after day, until we see a full moon, then it wanes and reduces in size from day to day. The phases of the moon, through its waxing and waning, teach us about life.

“You see,” said Elvis, “rise and fall, gain and loss, wax and wane are nothing but different phases and aspects of life. When the moon disappears, the sun appears.

“The old ways, cycles, and patterns remerged through different manifestations. You may not see it in your lifetime, but if you go back far enough in history, there’s nothing new under the sun. Study and learn from history.

“So don’t take yourself and life too seriously. When you add a bit of fun, laughter, and humor in your life, you will begin to experience more joy and peace,” Elvis laughed.

LESSON 8

The Art Of Being Mindful

"I have no idea what your work is like in human life," said Elvis.

"Well, we wear a suit, put on a tie, and tend to look more serious when we are at work," laughed Tom.

"Wonderful! You can remain calm with inner peace no matter what you do or how chaotic it may be in the external world. What matters is how you manage and guard your mind from the ever-changing external circumstances and distractions that surround you.

"Outwardly, imagine I put on a suit and a black tie, looking somewhat serious! I guess you need to do that for your practical human lives, to be effective and efficient. Inwardly, we experience joy and peace in our heart, and function from a place of wisdom." The panda reflects on this as he settles into a meditative posture, smiling.

Tom nodded in agreement, at the same time thinking about how one can maintain peace and serenity in the real world. "How can I feel peaceful when I am lost? How can I make peace in a situation when I'm in distress?"

"Breath! Learn to take up deep breathing. See our turtle friend there?" Elvis pointed to the turtle that moved slowly and lazily along the bank. "The turtle can live for a long time, as their breathing is long and deep."

"Yes, the turtle only takes maybe 2 to 3 breaths per minute. We humans average between 18 and 30 breaths per minute. It all depends on the condition of an individual. We can live without food and water for days, but not without breathing – without oxygen," Tom replied.

"The breath and the mind are interdependent. When your breath is long and deep, you feel calm. When your breath is shallow and irregular, you feel restless."

Elvis was indeed wise. “It seems as though, for you, breathing has become an incomplete, superficial, and hasty procedure. The action of breathing, for all living things, is a powerful driving force, and you can always feel better and think clearer when you focus on your breathing.”

“Is there a special way I should be doing this?” asked Tom.

“Right now, you are calm and at peace in your surroundings. You seem happy and your breathing is full and deep. When you need to relax, however, simply take deep and long breaths several times.”

Tom yawned. “I’m sorry. I am so chill in such a beautiful environment.”

Elvis laughed. “Yawning is a good sign. It shows that you are relaxed.”

Tom and Elvis continued their conversation.

“When you are in a stressful situation, take a few deep breaths to relax. Your emotions often cause stress, but it is a subjective experience. They are a product of how you perceive your world or a particular situation. Through the spectrum of emotions in your mind,” said Elvis, “you experience love or fear, and everything in between.

“You think, analyze and look at the outward world,” Elvis continued. “I allow, stay in the moment, and observe myself. There is a difference between a knowing – those things that come from the heart or are instinctual – and knowledge, which is either book-learned or taught to you by others.

"Let go of your past. Give up your worry for the future. Stay in the moment. Most often, you are in your thinking mind, when feeling is equally important. Move to the present moment by asking yourself, 'What am I feeling right now?' You function with your mind, but you must live with the wisdom of the heart as well."

Elvis continued, "Learn to be more mindful of your thoughts and emotions, without interpretation or judgment. Practice the art of mindfulness for a more peaceful life.

"During your busy life, sometimes we have to pause for a moment and just be. Your mind loves doing, yet there is a part of you that yearns to just do nothing. Humans feel this incessant need to constantly be productive to get ahead. But it's the balance between doing and being that makes one complete. Throughout the day, once in a while, take a deep breath and just be. When you put your mind to rest, you will find you become centered.

"Learn to meditate, calm your mind, and attain peace of mind. When you develop meditative awareness and focus on your breathing as a silent witness and without judgement – the inflows and outflows – you gradually become calm and put your mind at rest."

Tom began to become more aware of his state of mind, his thoughts, and how they affected him. He knew Elvis was right in this thinking, and he vowed to himself to practice mindfulness in his daily life.

Final Reflections

It was a cold evening. He was not sure he was capable of doing all that Elvis suggested, but he knew he would give his best. Perhaps he could incorporate these lessons into the stories he told the children. He did, however, greatly enjoy the company of Elvis and his wisdom. He hoped time could go on a little bit longer so he could stay here awhile.

"Night teaches us to engage a leap of faith into the unknown with fully knowing that we will be well and prevail, despite temporary setbacks. Learn to have faith and hope, because it's always darkest before the dawn. The thoughts you create today will be the reality you experience tomorrow, so make all your thoughts count; make them positive and happy.

"In regards to your past, learn to forget and forgive and move on with life." Elvis paused for a moment. “You know why I love bamboo so much? Because it keeps me drunk all day, and it helps cultivate a state of forgetfulness.”

Elvis continued, “In this journey, you have been trying to find the treasure. In fact, all the answers you seek are contained within. You can access this wisdom not through the mind, but through your heart.

“You pursue ‘knowledge’, when in fact ‘knowing’ is superior. That inward compass contains the true north and inner knowing. Somehow, you know deep in your heart who you want to become.

“It’s not so much that I have more wisdom to impart you, but with the hope that our conversation would stimulate greater awareness and self-understanding towards the fulfillment of your true destiny.”

As the panda spent half of his time sleeping and the other half eating, it was one of those times when he dozed off into his dream world and took a nap. The panda quickly and easily went into a deep sleep.

Looking at the night sky, Tom pondered on the various incidents and corresponding wisdom of the panda, for he marveled at the panda’s depth of insight, and examined his own way of living. He looked at the innocent wise panda and soon drifted into a deep slumber alongside him.

After a few hours, Elvis was now awake and observing Tom as he slept. He shook him gently. "You were smiling in your sleep. Did you have a nice dream?"

"Yes, friend, and I think I now understand all you have been trying to teach me. All happiness lies within us, and we each have the ability to create love and joy by first giving it away. When we give with joy and expect nothing in return, our joy multiplies."

"You honor me with your understanding. This wisdom is not mine but is mine to give. And I am grateful you have embraced my humble efforts."

The two friends continued to look up at the stars. They pondered its vast incomprehensible complexity while appreciating the simplicity of all things.

At first, Tom was anxious and restless to leave. Now he wanted to stay perhaps a little bit longer, to talk with Elvis and to reconnect with a part of himself that had been neglected for years; the feelings of his heart and his inner peace, and to experience what brought him joy.

Tom stared into the moonlight and vastness of the sky, quietly reflecting on the wisdom of the panda. The panda quickly fell asleep again.

The lessons inspired him with a renewed faith and hope for the future. He would now implement this newfound knowledge and wisdom in the real world so that his life would never be the same again.

The next morning, the sun rose clear and bright. As Tom arose and washed his face in a nearby stream and looked at the reflection of himself in the water, he noticed a difference and a shift within himself. He hadn't slept this well for many years, with peace and contentment in his heart, free from all anxiety and worry. He also saw the panda already enjoying his bamboo for breakfast.

"Thank you for your wise guidance and for imparting so much wisdom. I feel renewed and invigorated after our delightful conversation," Tom said cheerfully.

Elvis was pleased, and his eyes twinkled with wisdom and compassion. "I didn't offer you anything new. All that you encountered in this journey, the animal friends, nature, and our conversations, was to help you remember. Collectively, they serve as a mirror to what you already know in your heart and mind. The reflection of yourself you see in the water is a gentle yet powerful reminder. You have finally discovered the treasure and now realize it is inside of you. Nurture and develop it with your newfound wisdom.

"Now with this awakened
awareness, follow your heart,
and live your life in a new way.
Let your destiny unfold like the
flow of water in this stream,
with grace and effortless ease,
as nature intended.
Find, live, and fulfill
your true destiny."

The enlightening conversation between Elvis and Tom came to an end, but the friendship and lessons long remained in his heart. After all, it is not only about imparting lessons, but it is also a journey of remembrance. And the story doesn't end here, because it is a lifelong journey of self-understanding and self-actualization, towards the fulfillment of one's purpose and destiny.

The Author

Joseph Rodrick Law is an entrepreneur, investor, best-selling author, visiting professor, philanthropist, and Guinness World Record holder. Joseph serves as the Chairman and CEO of J Global Limited, a consulting firm that caters to private and public companies across various regions, including Australia, Hong Kong, China, Southeast Asia, India, the United States, and Europe. He also acts as an independent non-executive director for a financial company listed on the Stock Exchange of Hong Kong.

Joseph is the CEO of Chill Labs Artificial Intelligence Limited, a pioneer in the digital health industry with a vision to revolutionize human potential, through the fusion of modern science, ancient wisdom, and the power of artificial intelligence.

Joseph is recognized as an Amazon.com bestselling author and has served as a columnist for Forbes China and Marie Claire. He has penned two books, namely "The Chill Panda: Dealing with Change in Work and Life" and "Authentic Power and Greatness." Joseph's readership encompasses a diverse range of individuals, including influential business and political leaders, celebrities, royal families, and everyday people from around the world. Joseph has also been featured in interviews with renowned international media outlets such as Yahoo! Finance, Sky News, the Australian Financial Review, the Financial Times, and The Wall Street Journal.

Joseph was invited by The Honorable Bob Carr, the former Foreign Minister of Australia, to serve on the advisory board of the Australia-China Relations Institute at the University of Technology Sydney. He has collaborated with the Sustainable Stock Exchange Initiative, co-organized by the United Nations Conference on Trade and Development. He is a visiting professor at the School of Entrepreneurship in Rishihood University, India's first social impact university, headed by India's former Minister for Commerce & Industry.

Joseph frequently speaks at Fortune 500 companies such as J.P. Morgan, L'Oréal, Johnson & Johnson, and Optus, as well as leading universities. He has conducted interviews with individuals from diverse backgrounds, including heads of state, billionaires, CEOs, bestselling authors, celebrities, and a Nobel Prize laureate.

Joseph served as a judge for JUMPSTARTER, the esteemed Global Pitch Competition presented by the Alibaba Entrepreneurs Fund. He is also a member of the Cyberport Investor Network and a mentor for Cyberport, which is Hong Kong's flagship digital technology incubator for entrepreneurship, with over 2,000 companies. Furthermore, he acted as a mentor for the Tasmu Accelerator program by the Qatar Government.

Joseph holds the position of Chairman of the International Association of Mental Health Hong Kong and serves as the CEO of the JC Happiness Charity Foundation. These organizations are committed to promoting mental health awareness among the public and fostering love, creativity, and positive energy worldwide.

Books by Joseph Rodrick Law

Connect with Joseph

Joseph delivers timeless wisdom and practical guidance that empower you to overcome obstacles, unlock your full potential, and achieve lasting success in both life and work with clarity, resilience, and joy.

For exclusive access to Joseph's success insights, practical tools, and proven strategies—and to explore his latest books, courses, and upcoming events – visit his website.

Please visit: www.josephrodricklaw.com

Social Media

Website: www.josephrodricklaw.com

Facebook: www.facebook.com/JosephRodrickLaw

YouTube: www.youtube.com/c/JosephRodrickLaw

Instagram: www.instagram.com/JosephRodrickLaw

To contact Joseph: info@thechillpanda.com

Speaking Engagement

Joseph is a sought-after speaker who energizes and inspires audiences at international conferences, Fortune 500 companies, and top universities worldwide.

To invite Joseph as a keynote speaker for your next event, please contact us at: info@thechillpanda.com

Charity Foundations Co-Founded by Joseph

JC Happiness Charity Foundation

At the core of the JC Happiness Charity Foundation's mission lies the commitment to enhance peace, love, wisdom, health, and overall well-being on a global scale. From its inception, our vision was to establish a unique organization centered around core values of inclusion, sustainability, and a profound sense of purpose. Registered as a charitable institution in Hong Kong under Section 88 of the Inland Revenue Ordinance, the JC Happiness Charity Foundation aims to make a meaningful impact in the lives of 100 million people.

Website: www.jchappinesscharity.org
Contact: info@jchappinesscharity.org

International Association of Mental Health Hong Kong

The International Association of Mental Health Hong Kong is dedicated to addressing the challenges of mental health issues while fostering a happier and more sustainable global community. Dedicated to enhancing mental, physical, and spiritual well-being, the association is a driving force for positive change in the field of holistic health and wellness. Through its work in education, research, and mind-body healing practices, the organization serves as a beacon of transformation in the mental health landscape.

Website: www.mentalhealthhk.org
Email: info@mentalhealthhk.org

Guinness World Record

The Guinness World Record was achieved through a collaborative effort between the JC Happiness Charity Foundation and the International Association of Mental Health Hong Kong. In order to raise awareness about mental health, they launched the "INNER CHILL" campaign. This initiative saw the creation of over 18,000 pieces of The Chill Panda® art paintings by children and celebrities, which were showcased in 3,333 frames. The campaign aimed to amplify mental health awareness in the community while fostering love, creativity, and positive energy globally.

Both organizations are dedicated to shaping a better world by adhering to Environmental, Social, and Corporate Governance (ESG) principles and Sustainable Development Goals (SDG), emphasizing their commitment to sustainable practices and societal well-being.